FROM SHY *to* "OH MY!"

The Shy Introvert's Guide to Being Sexy, Expressive and Whole

Tyrus Gray

Copyright © 2020 by Tyrus Gray
All rights reserved

Cover art by Ryan Kent Paule

ISBN # 978-1-7347199-1-8

For YOU.

TABLE OF CONTENTS

- Expression is Expansion 1
- Nature 3
- Gender 4
- Religion 5
- Turning Point 6
- Stretch it Out 8
- Happening 10
- Presence 11
- How You Sound 13
- Looks 14
- Mirror Reflection 15
- Your Most Attractive 17
- Unashamed 20
- Into a Better Future 22
- Neither Introvert nor Extrovert 25
- Balance 27
- Flirting 29
- Eye Contact 32
- Make that Connection 34

Follow Up	39
Phone Calls	40
Chemistry	41
Accept a Sexy Response	42
Awaken	43
Sensational	45
Greatness through Gratitude	47
Confidence	49
Respect	51
Lighten Upward	53
Conversation is Sexy	54
Touch	56
Attention	57
Acceptance	58
Openness is Contagious	60
Free for All	62
Sincerity	63
Sharing Shyness	65
Sexual Strength	66
Release	68
Affirmations	69

Naughty Talk and Text	71
Clear Sharp Mind	74
Best Health	75
Whole Body	76
Be Someone to Be	77
Truth	79
Be Whole	80
Versions of You	81
Real Eyes	82
Initiate Intimacy	83
Smile Sexy	85
Feel What the Other Feels	86
Give	87
Stillness	89
Depressurize	91
Perfect	93
Role Play	94
Sex Not Required	96
Live	97
About the Author	98

CHAPTER ONE
Expression is Expansion

Allow your expression to fully represent you, and you engage with your sweetest opportunities.

I encourage you to decide, at this moment, to experience your most fulfilling life. Decide that the steps you take with this book will work wonderfully.

If you were shy through earlier stages of life, that shyness served an important purpose.

Many of us developed shyness as a way to preserve our truest sense of self. With instinctive wisdom, we hid our personality. We guarded our true expression from the effects of confusing, embarrassing or traumatic messages which we interpreted to be about ourselves.

Many of the habits we developed are no longer necessary. We can step out, now, from habits that limit our access to experiences we might find meaningful.

Your true expression has been kept pure,

powerful and ready!

Return to a sense of freedom that allows life to be how you want it to be.

Desirable experiences, such as intimate relationships, come easily when we allow expression that is without the contraction of self-judgement or fear. Your most radiant life happens when you relax into the expression that fully represents you.

Your life can be more exhilarating, fulfilling and sensual than you might even imagine.

Use this book to feel attractive and sexy, have fulfilling relationships, enjoy flirtation, have fun with sex, and become comfortable, confident and effective in all areas of life.

This book gives steps for immediate change. You will strengthen your natural expression, and allow an empowered ease toward having what is rightfully yours.

So . . .

Go from shy to "Oh, my!"

CHAPTER TWO
Nature

Our biology was likely designed for a more primitive time than where we find ourselves today. Nature compels the planet's species to populate their parts of the ecosystem. But in our current time, people might introduce a great deal of physical and emotional complications into their lives if they acted on every procreative urge.

Decide what you intend to create long-term with your choices. Choose to only be with those people who support your highest fulfillment. Guard your physical and emotional well-being. Only have romantic relationships when the situation will enrich your life.

Only the most supportive person, who has the highest integrity, may be worthy of your intimate affection. Never settle. Be picky.

CHAPTER THREE
Gender

This book will sometimes use pronouns such as "he" and "she" to refer to partners in a relationship. The information applies, just the same, if you are interested in a same sex relationship, or prefer other terms of identification.

Words are important. They influence our beliefs. I suggest we stop speaking about the different genders by calling one the "opposite sex." Healthy male and female energies do not oppose one another. They compliment.

CHAPTER FOUR
Religion

I grew up in Christian churches, where I absorbed countless religious teachings about sex. To this day, I value the messages about sex being sacred. I regret, however, the way I was led to feel ashamed and disconnected from sexual energies.

At an age when my sexuality was being revealed, I believed I needed to resist those "temptations." I recall trying to stop myself from even THINKING sexually! While my peers were awakening to the knowledge of their bodies, I tried to integrate the restrictive teachings of the church into my confused biology.

Viewing sex responsibly is an excellent lesson, at any age. But lessons that teach shame are unfortunate and wrong. Repression of our sexual and sensual nature can lead to blockages in many areas of our personalities and lives.

I invite you to be free from shame. This book has exercises to help.

CHAPTER FIVE
Turning Point

As a young adult, I saw my life devoid of close relationships. I was alone when I would have preferred to connect with another person. Romantic opportunities could have been available for me, but I felt unable to engage with them. I was too shy to take risks. Awkwardness took over my mind. I rarely pursued dating, and when I did, I did not come with confidence.

I became disengaged from life at the most fundamental level. I was not making myself attractive. I did not command what I wanted. I did not trust my own spontaneity.

I needed to free myself from self-limiting habits and beliefs. I needed to become confident and express myself.

A combination of simple choices began to reveal the techniques in this book. The most important truths came in an instant, as though an access code had been entered. I trust that these messages will also assist you as you gain access to your most fulfilling life.

CHAPTER SIX
Stretch it Out

Parts of my hips, thighs, groin and legs felt tight for most of my life. As an adult, I began stretching through these areas and realized a reason for the tightness. During a stretch, I would occasionally see images from my past surface in my mind. These were memories which had likely contributed to sexual confusion and repression. They had been stored in my body!

Stretch. Do not be concerned if memories and images surface momentarily out of the subconscious during the stretch. Relax into the truest, purest state of awareness, where you do not need to generate any emotional attachment to the memories. Let the memories and feelings be, and let them go.

Release.

Your word is your authority. You can speak to any part of your body. You may like to speak to your muscles while stretching, as a way to encourage, settle or rejuvenate them. You can similarly speak encouragement to your emotional body, anytime you choose.

Yoga offers a rich history of techniques to move into freedom with your body. Many of the stretches I find effective for releasing areas of sexual repression are not very exotic, and are stretches most people learn in early athletic environments, such as school gym class.

The sensation of stretching can become increasingly comfortable as you allow yourself to feel the stretch.

Walking — or any other physical activity that you enjoy — is also a great way to loosen from the past, shed what we no longer need, and integrate a helpful perspective.

CHAPTER SEVEN
Happening

All aspects of yourself can be seen as energy in motion. Who we are is not fixed nor stagnant. You choose the expression you get to be.

Decide which energies you will like to express. Your face, for example, can express as friendliness *happening*, beauty *happening*, confidence *happening*, or any other energies you prefer to set in motion. Your eyes might be influence *happening*, insight *happening*, sensuality *happening*, and so on. Your body might be enjoyment *happening*, strength *happening*, and whatever else you choose to have happen.

Express what you want, through all aspects of yourself.

CHAPTER EIGHT
Presence

Genuine connections come from being present and not withdrawn into fantasy.

To be present, be decidedly relaxed and open. Let curiosity replace judgement. Allow an unconditional self-love to override criticism of self. This approach creates a comfortable certainty for all areas of life.

In a romantic situation, bring a relaxed, receptive sensitivity to the experience. You do not need to cling to any specific, desired outcome. You do not need to be caught up in your thinking.

Show up and have a curiosity and willingness to experience joy. Be willing to have joy move through you.

Show you are open. Show you care for a lover or potential lover, as well as for yourself. Slow down. To the right person, your body will broadcast an instinctive invitation into life's sweetness.

There is power when we move beyond the

drifting fantasies of our own minds, and become fully present with someone. This presence lets you feel the signals coming from the person, as though you speak a silent, secret language.

By being present, you are your most attractive and inspired self.

CHAPTER NINE
How You Sound

If you need to sound more confident when speaking with others, here are suggestions you can practice:

Visualize expansion at the areas where your voice sounds. You can imagine that your speech is being welcomed by both the earth and sky. This allows a fullness of voice to come through. It can also help you to feel grounded and inspired, simultaneously.

Energize your speech by intending to *give* through your voice to the people with whom you speak. Do not overthink your voice. Just be willing to give an uplifted mood, as though it were an invisible, secret gift.

Also, eliminate the use of words and phrases which sound uncertain. These might include "maybe," "I guess," "I don't know," "umm," and so on. You do not need to pretend to know everything. Just speak as directly as you can.

CHAPTER TEN
Looks

Advertisers have no shame about making people feel inadequate. They pollute our mental landscape for the purpose of creating their market of customers. But we can avoid that trap! The true image of beauty is YOU!

A lover must be able to cherish you exactly as your are.

Cherish yourself.

You are perfect. You do not need to match a certain physical criteria to be the sexiest creation ever. You are it.

You embody all the seductive power the world has ever seen.

CHAPTER ELEVEN
Mirror Reflection

Realize your seductive power by taking time to gaze into a mirror. Be with your reflection until you become aware of your sexual attractiveness. Get to know what a lover will feel when he or she appreciates and craves you. Do this without judgement. The attraction is not based on any superficial comparisons. Accept yourself.

As you gaze, you can repeat a word that represents what you intend to communicate with your appearance. This could be a word like "sexy," "strong," "natural," "beautiful," or any other words that feel right to you. As you repeat the word, see your posture and countenance shift to align with the message, as though every part of you knows exactly what to do.

You can correct areas of your body where you had appeared withdrawn. Look yourself over. Do you appear to be withholding parts of your body from the reflected image? Do you observe that your eyes are set back, mouth clenched in, hips not positioned as prominent, or your chest or face is angled downward? Do you see other ways you positioned yourself as withdrawn? Practice presenting yourself as simultaneously comfortable and powerful. You are seen as attractive when you can bring your full presentation to another person.

Smile for an unusually long time at your reflection. Smile until you actually begin to feel like smiling. At this point, a shift can occur, and you will see your smile change to appear very natural. Doing this may feel strange, but stick with it over time. We begin to feel happy and comfortable with ourselves.

Your eyes can be expressive. Learn to "smile" with your eyes, by bringing a great smile to your whole face, and then back off every physical aspect of the expression except for your eyes. This means you smile and then bring the muscles and shape of your mouth and face back to a mostly neutral position, except keep only your eyes "smiling." Your eyes, then, maintain their warmth and allure.

"Smiling" using only your eyes is a skill you can use to engage someone to want to connect with you, without your needing to demonstrate any overt type of advance.

CHAPTER TWELVE
Your Most Attractive

A potential lover is often more interested in how you make him or her feel, than how impressive you make yourself sound. You make great headway by being attentive to the person.

Hear what the person says. Respond.

Fellas, when you are with a woman whom you like, appreciate where she gives special attention in life. Ask an additional question — any question — when you pick up on her interest in some subject matter. Be interested.

Ladies, when you are speaking with a man whom you like, communicate your approval when you like his choices. Affirm that you like the details of his plans. Show approval, and he may warm up to you very quickly.

Fellas, you need to be comfortable making plans. We shy and introverted people have sometimes felt uncomfortable choosing activities — or even speaking with someone to make plans — but demonstrating your planning ability will assure a potential lover of your willingness to care for her. Even the smallest of plans can have this positive effect. If asking for a date, speak to her with specificity, with something like, "There is a place I'd like to try with you, and I hear the best time is early in the evening, so will you join me Friday evening at 6? I can pick you up."

I remember being young and terribly naive. I would intend to spend time with a romantic interest, but would show up without much consideration of where to go or what to do. My level of attractiveness dropped down to around zero. I later learned how having a plan would have given much different results!

Have a plan and a backup plan.

After a long time with one partner, there can develop a tendency to relax and do *whatever*. But you should continue to keep a schedule of planned dates. Again, the plans can be very simple. The point is that you considered, ahead of time, what sounds fun to experience together.

Ladies, you can let yourself be viewed as physically alluring, even if you felt modest about your appearance in the past. A lover will like to see you confidently show glimpses of your sexuality. You might choose to dress with a flirtatious intent when you are with him. A subtle sexiness — as though the tight outfit were your "usual" for an evening around the house — is often more powerful than any overt display, so no need to get carried away.

Even small changes can have a tremendous effect. Be deliberate with what you communicate in your choices of clothing, grooming, cleanliness, and actions. Be seen as your most attractive self.

CHAPTER THIRTEEN
Unashamed

In our history, all that was done up until now — by you and by others — represents the levels of awareness that each person had at that time.

One way we can heal *from* the past is to *heal* the past.

Some of our choices may not have been ideal, but who you truly are has always been perfect. Rescue your perfect self from the past. You can offer love and encouragement to your memories. To those past versions of yourself, you can say, "You are perfect," whether from years, days, or minutes ago. You may like to repeat that statement several times.

Who you are right now *is* your perfect self rescued from the past.

Mistakes show the ways which we needed to heal. Give healing comfort and perspective to those past versions of yourself, from your wiser, current state of awareness. Realize how you were always perfect in your deepest essence.

You have always been pure. Let nothing obscure that purity from your identity. Let no one obscure it from you.

Forgiveness is helpful if you have been harmed. Please do not suppose I am tasking anyone with making a great emotional leap toward forgiveness. Hurt can hurt. Our guard goes up and stays up for a reason. But you can choose how you want to live. Live so deliberately that the memory from the harmful, dysfunctional person or situation is no longer relevant to your reality. You are discerning. You are safe.

Who you are has a perfect purpose.

CHAPTER FOURTEEN
Into a Better Future

Uncomfortable memories, addictions, uneasiness, or unhealthy habits or beliefs, no longer need to influence you. Free your mind and emotional body with this imaginative exercise.

I will include a lot of details, but the process is very simple, and can be done in seconds, at any time, once you are familiar with it:

1. Imagine you have a very unique photo album book. All parts of the book (the cover, pages and binding) are transparent. You hold it up and can see right through it. The book is magical, in a way, since anything that goes into it also becomes transparent.
2. Notice you are in your most idyllic setting. You do not need to be specific about the details of the place, just have it feel pleasant. For example, I might imagine a peaceful forest, or a beach with an emerald green sea

with sunlight sparkling upon it. Choose any setting you like.

3. Take a look at your setting through the transparent album, as you hold the book up in your hands.
4. Open the book to one of the clear pages. The backing page is like a heavy card stock, but is totally transparent. A thin plastic protective sheet adheres to the backing page, and can be peeled back to place a picture onto the page, much like a traditional photo album.
5. Peel back one of the plastic sheets, and leave it ready for the placement of an image.
6. Consider any habit, memory, thought, belief or pattern that had been uncomfortable, shameful, toxic, wearisome, or unhelpful in any way, and imagine you now have an image of it in on a card. Hold that card with your hand. You may see the image on the card as a picture or as text. The card may, at first, appear in your hand, or you may need to reach and grab it from nearby or inside of you. The card may be located somewhere like your head or solar plexus, so you can imagine reaching into an area of your body and pulling it out.
7. Remember, whatever goes into this book

becomes clear. Place the card onto the page and reapply the thin plastic sheet overtop it.
8. Watch the entire card become transparent. You may notice the image on the card desaturate to appear black and white, as it fades into total transparency. As it fades, you can see more of your idyllic setting through the clear page, if you hold up the book. If the transparent clarity happens only slowly, you can imagine holding the book up to where the sun shines through it, and observe the transparency process become helped by the sunshine.
9. Smile at the magical album, which has returned to being totally clear. Look around, again, at your ideal scene. You can now set down the book and walk away.

CHAPTER FIFTEEN

Neither Introvert nor Extrovert

We shy people tend to think, speak and act from an introverted point of reference. I do not advise changing, however, from being an introvert to becoming an extrovert. While neither state is wrong, both introversion and extroversion can lead to an incomplete perception of the world.

The introvert is susceptible to sinking into an unreal inner world of thoughts and feelings. The extrovert is susceptible to grasping at an unreal outer world.

I suggest you bring your awareness of self to the point between any apparent inner and outer worlds. See how both the inner and outer worlds blossom from your truth when you are affected by neither. You allow perfect peace into your inner sense of feeling. You allow perfect opportunities into your outer experience.

Relax and allow what is right for you. People have their bodies made right through the relaxation of sleep. You can have your circumstance made right by relaxing with it.

If your relaxed expression ends up seeming quirky by society's standards, know that the perceived quirkiness will also work to your advantage. You need to be you.

CHAPTER SIXTEEN
Balance

Feeling balanced allows you to have stability and strength. When you feel stable and strong, you easily present your most attractive self.

We tend to express the types of attributes that we appreciate in life, so appreciate the pleasant nature of balance whenever and wherever you can. Our world has many creations that demonstrate a harmonious balance of qualities.

Many types of cuisine have a pleasant balance of flavor profiles. Find a food or drink you enjoy for the complexity of combined flavor profiles, and really experience it. Indian food is one example where you tend to have multiple flavor profiles in balance, like when there is a collective flavor which manages to be both spicy and sweet. Certain fruits, chocolates, beers, coffees, wines, or other foods and drinks will have a complex balance of different flavors. Experience the different flavor profiles together as one. Appreciate the balance.

Your homework, then, is to eat or drink something tasty!

Be your own pleasant balance of qualities. All aspects of you are valuable. They can be present, in harmony, for your most fulfilling life.

Being one dimensional does not create a longevity of attractiveness. For example, someone's humor could become wearisome if the light-heartedness were not also balanced with a quality such as sincerity. Physical beauty can begin to seem unattractive unless balanced with other qualities such as a sense of purpose. Sexyness can even become uninviting if not balanced with other qualities.

Your personal attributes come together as a whole. That whole is greater than the sum of its parts. Now, you are the tasty dish!

We are metaphorically identifying the difference between a generic lollipop and an expert tiramisu. Be the tiramisu! Or, perhaps choose to be a tiramisu lollipop if that sounds like the most fun — whatever best represents you and the experience you will like to have!

CHAPTER SEVENTEEN
Flirting

Flirting means you let someone begin to feel the fun you might have together. You reveal your personality.

If you try what you believe to be flirting but are not having fun — or feel you are not being true to yourself — stop. Meaningful flirtation is always fun and genuine.

You do not need to score points in a flirtatious conversation. The conversation should not be considered a fearful game that can be lost. Let it be play in which everyone wins.

Do not attempt to manipulate anyone into liking you. You simply give the opportunity for the right person to be in your presence and fall for you.

Compliments can be fun for anyone. Many "pickup artists" caution men against giving compliments, but approval is powerful. An honest compliment using the word "I," can open up a connection. You might say, "I am happy to see someone so patient," to the woman who is handling difficult customers at her workplace, or "I like talking with you," or any other genuine compliment you phrase in this way. When you show approval, the person can begin to wonder what else you might like.

Keep in mind, an attractive person may not be especially moved by hearing that she or he is attractive, so be creative with what you say.

Banter can sometimes feel intimidating to shy and introverted people. We do not like for a conversation to feel frenetic. But on the other hand, a friendly form of banter may serve an important purpose when meeting someone. You can use banter, and all forms of communication, to show your personality. When meeting a man, a woman may want to get a quick read on him. She wants to get a sense of his intelligence, humor, and how confident he can be with her. She may choose to accomplish this in the quickest way possible: banter. Do not resent this opportunity.

Have you ever thought of the "right thing" to say to someone long after you left the conversation? We all have. Usually, the perfect response comes to us later in the bathroom or in bed or wherever we finally relaxed. You can access this witty ability in an instant when you let yourself relax with the person. Your natural personality and wit will come through.

Treat everyone the same. This helps us feel relaxed and stable when we do interact with someone we find attractive.

If you are feeling an especially sexual response from the person, you can imagine you are relaxing *into* him or her by way of the conversation. This state of mind can make the communication feel very sexy, no matter what you are saying.

We will explore another powerful form of flirting, in the next chapter.

CHAPTER EIGHTEEN
Eye Contact

You are seen as confident when you can make eye contact. If you make eye contact with someone and both appear to be enjoying the moment, you can be seen as alluring when you stay with that point of contact.

Begin to experiment with keeping eye contact for slightly longer than usual. To keep from looking away too quickly, use the moment to let your eyes convey approval of the other person. This unspoken approval may feel very warm and valuable to him or her.

Men appear especially confident by maintaining eye contact for a slightly longer duration than the woman. I have observed many couples where the man is considered a confident person. When the confident man meets the eyes of his lover, he will typically not look away until after she has done so. When he does look away, he almost never looks downward.

During eye contact, you can experiment with taking a single breath through a slightly opened mouth, and then return to your normal breathing. This can plant a sexual suggestion. Similarly, a single glance down at the other person's mouth can suggest intimacy.

Having been introverted or shy, we rarely need to worry about coming on too strong. Even if eye contact feels awkward at first, it may not appear awkward to anyone else. A light smile on your face can help you remain comfortable.

Eye contact can strengthen all areas of your connection with a person. It is not only for prompting sex, but do not be surprised if your lover starts reaching for your body when you do make strong eye contact.

During foreplay and sex, eye contact can get the erotic feelings to surge. Sex does not require any specific amount of eye contact, but I encourage you to experiment with including a little more, then be ready for a pleasant surprise.

Remember to let your eyes "smile."

CHAPTER NINETEEN
Make that Connection

If you see someone you will like to meet, let yourself perceive what that person is experiencing at that moment. Perceive this as fully as you can by setting aside your own intentions. Speak from a place of willingness to understand him or her, and you can intuitively say what will be comfortable and best suited for the person to hear.

When saying an opening line or introduction, do not be random. Only bring up an idea that may already be in the person's awareness. Your initial connection should present yourself as connected with the person's mind. Do not, for example, try to strike up a conversation about some far-off object, or obscure fact, when s/he would not have already been thinking about that thing. Some people believe randomness of speech is clever, but it can be disorienting upon first meeting. Non sequiturs can also make a stranger appear to be out of touch with reality.

Having no opening line can be to your advantage. You show bravery by just coming over to the person with a willingness to connect.

Do not pretend to experience a connection with someone. If you are not *vibing* with the person, you can move on.

Fellas, you can develop your natural ability to communicate by deciding to talk to people regularly, and not just the people you find attractive. Communicate messages of encouragement to anyone, whenever you can. You do not need to impress people with what you say. Just genuinely wish the best for others, and let that message come across. This may not always mean you give a compliment. Sometimes, you might just show how you are impressed with the person during your interaction.

Ladies, you may choose to be more reserved around male strangers, and not strike up random conversations, if you need to avoid their getting the wrong idea. But you can make a habit to talk and connect with those whom you are comfortable or would like to meet. When you are interested in someone, remember, a smile and eye contact are very compelling to initiate further interaction.

You can ask a question to the person. Most people feel good about being helpful or sharing an opinion. Be appreciative of the answer, and see if he or she wants to continue talking.

When you are with someone whom you might like to know better, you can aim your eyes where they can be met. If eye contact is held for a few seconds, the person may like to share some time getting acquainted.

You can be approachable when you open your body toward the person, especially the area of your heart, and direct it toward him or her. Do this as much as feels right. Ladies, this simple shift of body language can make the guy want to walk right over.

Remember, people may be in the midst of all kinds of experiences which have nothing to do with you as they go about their day. You can simply be open to the possibility of getting acquainted if the circumstance is right.

If you become curious to meet someone but he or she is scrolling around on a cellphone, do not assume the person is too busy for your introduction. Fifteen years ago, a person crunching data on a phone was probably doing important work. Nowadays, though, most phone use is simply meant to pass time. Go ahead and approach. The person may be happy that you did.

If you will be at a place where you might like strangers to talk with you, you can carry or wear some type of conversation item. This could be a t-shirt of a favorite movie, a meaningful piece of jewelry, a book, or just about anything else. Choose an item that sets you apart. If you wear a movie t-shirt, for example, someone may spot it and only be intersted in discussing the director's cut or sequel or any other related details. But just as often, someone may start a conversation because he or she is interested in what is under the shirt…you know, the heart.

You can bring helpers onto your team. If there are friends or family whom you trust, describe your ideal partner to them. Who knows? They may have a hot match-making idea.

You can give yourself a mathematical advantage by how you choose to spend your time. As a shy person, I have known many times of solitude. My hobbies and habits can seem isolating (hey, I am happily hidden away writing this book). But if we go weeks without meeting anyone new, we are less likely to connect with someone we may like, than if we are meeting new people regularly. Would you like to meet people through volunteering with a group or charity? Would you enjoy attending meet-up groups with people who share an interest in your otherwise solitary hobbies? Would you like to attend a church? Consider which activities appeal to you. You might simply take a book to a coffee shop instead of reading it on the living room couch.

You do not need to focus heavily on meeting someone. You can lighten up about that area of life. Do what you love and love follows. Most of life follows a win-win equation. By doing what you enjoy, you have fun and are also seen in the most attractive way by others.

Be open when the time is right. Smile a big, assured smile for no reason. Give positivity.

CHAPTER TWENTY
Follow Up

When you talk with someone, he or she may share details which you can file away for later. If you follow up with a text message or call, or when you see the person again, ask about something which was mentioned previously. You show your interest, and he or she will likely appreciate how you were listening.

Your life — and your mind — may be busy, but show you are willing to make genuine space for the person.

CHAPTER TWENTY-ONE
Phone Calls

Many people will be inclined to send text messages instead of making a call. But you can set yourself apart when you pick up the phone and call a potential lover.

Don't plan to remain on the call indefinitely. After you have a pleasant exchange, have a reason why you need to hang up. You might say there is an important task you are off to handle.

You show the person how you wanted to connect more deeply than you might have by only sending a text.

Fellas, if you think the woman is sought after by other suitors, calling may position yourself more deeply into her imagination. The other guys only sent texts, but you were bold.

CHAPTER TWENTY-TWO
Chemistry

Let your sexual presence assert itself to a lover or potential lover. This only asks that we suspend any insecurities of the mind, then show up. Do not stay in your head with reservations about letting yourself be seen. Chemistry happens naturally. Allow it.

To help bring your sexual presence to someone, get in touch with your desire to be close with him or her. Let the activity of feeling surpass the activity of thought. You feel the current of energy, then silently invite the other person to feel it. Often times, the sexiest thing you can do is position yourself right in front of the person, then let your chemistries do what they will.

CHAPTER TWENTY-THREE
Accept a Sexy Response

Insecurities can spread a haze over our perception of reality. Someone could intend to communicate a sexually inviting message to you, but you need to be comfortable accepting that sort of attention to not miss it.

Accept that you will be an amazing gift in the life of your perfect lover.

Realize that your lover will want to see you as sexy. He or she will want to be seen as sexy, as well.

CHAPTER TWENTY-FOUR
Awaken

To get in touch with your sexual energy, find time away from others when you can make sounds without feeling self-conscious.

Produce a series of deep, bursting "Uhh!" sounds with your voice. Feel the vibration of the sound. See if you can allow even more primal sounds to come from your mouth, as you also allow your body to shake in a pleasant sense of release. Can you feel the sound vibrations in areas of your body? Do you feel the vibration in your stomach? Can you feel it through your pelvic area? Can you feel it in your feet? Do not be concerned with how the vocalizations sound. The point is to experience your sexual energy that originates inside you.

Let your expression be free.

You may also choose to jump or lunge your body during the vocalizations. You can do this in pleasurable bursts that also release tension.

Similarly, you can become accustomed to

elevated moods by making spontaneous, joyful sounds, the way a soulful singer might become spontaneous while singing a powerful, rhythmic song. The singer throws his or her voice into the pleasurable vibrations, making vocal sounds like:

"Oh!"

"Yeah!"

"Hah!"

Pretend for a moment that by just being alive, your life is the greatest, most harmonious, rhythmic, musical jam. Let joyful sounds fly out of you. There are secrets in the joyful tones. The keys are actual *keys*. Unlock your good mood.

CHAPTER TWENTY-FIVE
Sensational

You can be more naturally sensual as you allow an increased awareness of physical sensations throughout your day. Whether you are scrubbing your skin, walking in the sun, or engaged in any activity, experience what you feel (and feel what you experience).

While drinking water, be open to the possibility that a single sip may hold the greatest level of refreshment the world has ever ever felt. A single breath might carry the deepest peace ever experienced by centuries of meditating monks.

Will you open yourself to feeling sensations? What if you did and every moment of life, no matter how mundane, could have immeasurable pleasure?

People tend to enjoy fine luxuries because they let themselves be present for those experiences. The chocolate connoisseur allows for a deep experience when tasting a fine chocolate. The wine lover gives full attention to the sip of a world-class wine. The art lover stands in awe at the Sistine Chapel. What few people know, however, is that the joy in those experiences is mainly due to our presence, and does not necessarily depend on the object of the chocolate or wine or art or whatever else.

To help yourself be present for a fullness of sensation, you can communicate with anything you experience. As an example, today at breakfast, I ate a waffle. I was enjoying the waffle, but began to wonder if I was fully experiencing the sensation. I decided to ask the waffle, "Waffle, what will you be for me?" The waffle, right then, became very delicious, as though it were eager to clarify the fullest experience of texture and flavor that a waffle can give. I expressed my gratitude.

Science is beginning to identify how all matter is effectively energy which shows up to meet our intended purpose. Go ahead and expect every aspect of life to meet you for your sensual enjoyment.

As we open to the richness of each moment, our lives can change. We experience life more fully. We also develop our ability to communicate sensuality.

CHAPTER TWENTY-SIX
Greatness through Gratitude

Gratitude builds our connection to life.

I mentioned my showing appreciation to a waffle. I could become even more specific with that appreciation. I might thank the ingredients like the grains that grew, the sun that shone down, and every aspect of life that came to support my health and experience.

As we show appreciation, we begin to see how our fulfillment is supported by life. We connect with clarity.

The tough question may arise: how do we feel grateful when we dislike what we are experiencing? Please know that any circumstance — as well as our history — is the precise launching ground for us to elevate into our sweetest, most enjoyable experience. If you are reading this, right now, you are showing life that you are ready to live in a way that is joyful and whole. We can be grateful to be right where we are, which is moving into our true perfection.

CHAPTER TWENTY-SEVEN
Confidence

Shy people are sometimes viewed as lacking confidence. This assumption is unfortunate. With a few simple choices, though, we can be seen as more confident.

Confidence is conveyed when you remove the potential for self doubt from the equation of your thinking. Your sense of worth is never on the line. Know you are always divinely perfect. No matter what experiences you currently navigate, the purity of your spirit lets you sail to the ideal place.

Confidence is demonstrated by integrity of character. Care about the commitments in your life. Focus on what is important to you. When you are not seeking self-importance, your genuine sense of purpose can be seen, and you are recognized in your greatness.

You do not need to take on a false personality.

Small modifications to our behavior can bring large changes to how we are seen. As shy or introverted people, we may act reserved in how we express ourselves. Experiment with adding a little more volume to your voice. If this feels strange, ask someone whom you trust to tell you whether or not you sound natural. You may be surprised. Much of what feels bold to us can seem ordinary to everyone else. When we learn this, we can have fun being a bit more bold, then perhaps, a lot more bold.

You are also seen as confident when you do what you want to do. Act without overthinking. If you want to show a form of affection — and you have confirmation that it would be welcomed — act! This also applies to what we do in all areas of life. We do not need to overthink. Do what is right for you without putting anything off.

Get to enjoy life.

CHAPTER TWENTY-EIGHT
Respect

If a person is rude, belittling, or disrespectful in any way, their behavior is not a statement about who you are. The person is only showing his or her own limited capacity for connection.

You are to be valued and respected. Respond immediately from this truth to steer yourself into a better situation.

Many of us have tended to quietly let things be said and done by others, even when we dislike what was communicated. We hear something that does not feel right, then attempt to understand, and often end up overthinking our response while the other person just moves on. But a simple, immediate, and strong response is typically all that is needed.

People who allow their own spontaneity have a major advantage at stopping disrespect. Responding to disrespect by immediately saying something like "no, no, no…" or "really?!" or "that's not what I'm about," or "I'm not okay with that," can be enough to show you disapprove of what has been presented to you. You show that you are someone who only accepts respect. If necessary, you could proceed to explain how you felt, as long as the person is receptive and is *on your side*.

Stay away — or get away — from people who treat anyone in a heartless way. We may have believed that a particular person would be thoughtful and warm toward us, even though he or she can be seen to demonstrate a disrespect for others. A disrespectful person, though, relies on selfishness. That selfishness would eventually bring toxicity your way.

If someone seems disrespectful, manipulative or narcissistic, you can save yourself a great deal of time by stopping all interactions with the person. A permanent correction may be appropriate, where you totally remove yourself from his or her influence. Move on with your better and truer life.

Make respect a priority.

CHAPTER TWENTY-NINE
Lighten Upward

You can bring a lighthearted assurance into your state of feeling. Smile and laugh throughout the day, especially to yourself.

Know that everything will be alright.

CHAPTER THIRTY
Conversation is Sexy

Most people will consider conversation to be an essential energetic exchange for having a relationship.

When you like someone, let yourself say something. What you say does not entirely matter. What matters is the energetic mood you choose to give with your speech. This mood serves as the base of the communication. Do you choose to promote an ecstatic experience for the other person?

Be open. Let your lover into your mind by speaking freely.

Listen without judgement.

Allow conversation to be an activity where you be yourself.

To let conversation come more naturally, practice. Speak to yourself around the house, or during a walk out in nature. You may also experience a sense of catharsis when you open up in this way.

Here is an idea that may sound silly, but can work wonders. As a practice, you can talk with a stuffed animal. Explain yourself to your stuffed friend. Share your thoughts and feelings. Many of us did this as children. It is especially helpful at making us comfortable with having someone be receptive to us.

CHAPTER THIRTY-ONE
Touch

When you are talking with a potential lover, be aware of moments when his or her expression enlivens. She or he may smile, laugh, and appear happy about talking with you. When you notice such a high point in the conversation, you might like to touch briefly. The quick, light touch, like somewhere on an arm or hand, at a high moment of the conversation, can innocently introduce the idea of intimacy. You plant an association in the person's mind between the fun you are having with conversation and the fun you could be having in a more physical way.

CHAPTER THIRTY-TWO
Attention

Have you noticed how countless societal entities want your attention? Social media sites want to have your eyes all day long. Content creators want your views. Many celebrities want you to watch their lives. Your attention is the most valuable resource on the planet.

Bringing your attention entirely to a lover or potential lover is a wonderful gift. It can generate the fullest erotic experience. Pause all self-referential thoughts, be totally present, and see what happens.

CHAPTER THIRTY-THREE
Acceptance

Acceptance of a lover can be communicated at all times. You can also plan a specific time to sit together in a session where you directly affirm acceptance of one another.

The planned session can begin by describing any insecurity you had in your life. For example, I might share how being short had me feel overlooked and disrespected by people in my life, and so on. As you share past insecurities, you each show total acceptance and love. Speak that acceptance and love. "Even though I felt insecure about my height, I give complete acceptance and love to myself." Your lover will also communicate complete acceptance and love to you.

You are perfect. Let your lover know she or he is perfect. Show acceptance with your words and your eyes. You need no judgement.

Cast away any messages you once held which made you feel uncomfortable or lacking. Those lies will stop coming around. Say to yourself, "I only accept messages of encouraging truth!"

You can also say, "I am whole! I accept my perfect life experience!"

Be seen as perfect by your lover and yourself.

CHAPTER THIRTY-FOUR
Openness is Contagious

Being open encourages the other person to also open up.

If you developed a sense of uneasiness earlier in life around the concepts of closeness or trust, you can have conversations with a potential lover to determine if the person deserves your trust. Is he or she dependable in all the ways you require, 100 percent of the time, to all people? You may want to move slowly and take time to see if the person's behavior affirms a strong commitment to the relationship. Get a sense of how other people view your potential lover, especially those people who have known him or her over a long period of time. Take time to check in with what is true about the relationship.

Openness happens through what we choose to say and reveal. It happens with our body language. It also happens through our willingness to listen.

Will you be vulnerable? Is the relationship

worthy of your vulnerability? Being open helps us become close with the right person.

CHAPTER THIRTY-FIVE
Free for All

Let's consider an imaginary scenario. Pretend that every person in the world has come peacefully to you in a large gathering (yes, the sight of the crowd would extend for as far as the eye can see). The people have genuine, honest expressions on their faces. They came to ask you a sincere question. They ask:

"Will you please be free? Your freedom will mean freedom for all the world!"

Each of us would most likely embrace the opportunity to heal the world in this way. Our own freedom would give us a sense of pride, knowing it would also give equal benefit to that entire crowd of people.

This hypothetical situation precisely represents our actual situation. Our own healing and freedom will benefit all of the world.

CHAPTER THIRTY-SIX
Sincerity

Many people in of our culture feel jaded. People hide behind cynical jokes. Open hearted conversations become rare.

I urge you to be who you are. Speak genuinely. Show appreciation of other people, and appreciate yourself.

Know that all aspects of you are all right. The different parts of your personality provide helpful abilities. Each can be applied in healthy ways toward having your most fulfilling life.

You can know what is best for you. Your awareness is like the needle of a compass that goes directly to what is healthy and fulfilling for you. That needle does not swing around to glance back in the direction of past mistakes or toward times when you were not being your best self. That needle does not keep glancing over at other people's follies. You look to the life you choose to enjoy.

Your authenticity will show to others. Someone who is ready for a true, fulfilling connection will feel welcomed by your sincerity.

CHAPTER THIRTY-SEVEN
Sharing Shyness

If you decide to reveal any personal challenges regarding shyness to a lover or potential lover, you can communicate in a way that shows strength and resolve. For example, I might say, "I'd like you to know that I've had tendencies toward shyness, but I am committed to do everything I can to have healthy communication." Do not describe a problem. Nothing needs to be viewed as a problem. Use the discussion as an opportunity to share your commitment to positive choices.

If you want assistance moving out of a behavior, your lover should have the maturity to understand and assist you. If you say something like, "I am trying to be more of myself. Help me to be me," he or she should meet you with love, understanding and support.

CHAPTER THIRTY-EIGHT
Sexual Strength

You may choose to strengthen your sexual ability by exercising the muscles through your body's pelvic floor. These are often called "Kegel muscles," named after the gynecologist who provided a great deal of research. You develop the ability to contract the muscles. You control the tightening, hold the contraction, and comfortably control the release.

You may experience your sensation of control as a tightening, lifting or squeezing together of the muscle group.

The exercises engage the pelvic floor muscles in the way you would if you were trying to stop or slow the flow of urine, or were perhaps holding back both flatulence and urine. You can exercise them, though, at almost any time when you do not need to urinate.

Fellas, exercising these muscles can strengthen your sexual functioning for dependable erections.

Experiment with what is comfortable and gives you the most control.

Ladies, you can bring deep enjoyment for both you and your lover by exercising these muscles. You gain the ability to control the sensations during sex.

Begin this discovery process with a bit of patience. The feeling of control may be subtle at first. Be aware of the slightest sensations, and continue to practice. At some point in time, you probably gained the ability to pucker the lips of your mouth. You will soon be able to perform the contraction of the pelvic muscles, in the same way.

The pelvic area of the human body is our point of origin into life in this world. The area can be seen as bridging Earth and heaven. You can experience a depth of positive feeling by simply becoming aware of these muscles and engaging them.

CHAPTER THIRTY-NINE
Release

You can experience a great sense of physical and emotional release with this variation of a pelvic muscles exercise:

1. Begin by tightening the muscles through the pelvic floor. When you achieve the tightened contraction, begin to also tighten any additional muscles throughout your entire body. You might tighten the muscles through your legs, face, fingers, feet, stomach, and anywhere you can bring your awareness.
2. Continue breathing.
3. With all the muscles tightened, release first the pelvic muscles, with gentle control.
4. In that moment, when the pelvic muscles relax, allow all the other bodily muscles to follow in an effortless release and relaxation.

CHAPTER FORTY
Affirmations

Speaking repeated affirmations can direct us into our most enjoyable, truest sense of self.

Read through this brief description, then you may like to begin exercising an affirmation.

Set a timer to last for at least 44 seconds, then use that time to repeat a spoken message to yourself, such as:
 "I accept myself completely,"
  "All energies serve my perfect life,"
  "I am living my very best life,"
  "I naturally express as confident,"
  Or, any other belief you will like to integrate as your own expression.
If you begin to feel or hear contradictory messages in your mind, just continue to speak your positive affirmation. Imagine that all of Creation begins to speak your affirmation with you, as if sounding in

a great harmonization of tones.

You can speak affirmations using a full voice or a whisper. When we whisper, we create a rich spectrum of tones, similar to how white light includes a full spectrum of colors.

You can choose to repeat the affirmation rapidly. Rapid speech may help reveal if a word or theme is butting up against a subconscious blockage. Push through to the point of fluency with what you speak. My speech has sometimes seemed unnatural, anyway, due to shyness, so this practice has the added benefit of helping speech flow more naturally for me.

Affirmations often start with the word "I," but you may experiment with variations and see how you feel. As a variation, you can speak your name instead of saying "I." When you do this, you might even imagine you are hearing other people say these complimentary statements about you.

CHAPTER FORTY-ONE
Naughty Talk and Text

To increase the sexual charge in your relationship, you might consider experimenting with naughty talk, either verbally or by text. First, though, look at your relationship and make sure you are being available to your lover on all levels. Sex is usually best when it comes as the culmination of your entire connection.

Naughty talk or texts do not need to happen all of the time. It may have the greatest impact if it is unexpected.

If you feel like generating a naughty mood during your time together, like on a dinner date at a restaurant, do not be too quick to introduce naughty talk. Be available. Hear about his or her day. Check in on the dreams and ambitions of each other. Support a positive sense of self. Talk about school or work or whatever else. When you feel especially unified — and if no one else is within earshot — you might choose to heighten the sexual mood by speaking a quick, naughty thought.

In the right moment, the sexy communication can be fun for your lover to process. It feels especially naughty when you are in public with no opportunity — nor expectation — to respond in a physical way. You build an exciting tension. Your lover may choose to return to the idea later.

Use a statement that can spark your lover's imagination. Be sure to follow up with a naughty smile.

Speaking an erotic idea may seem challenging if we have been shy about talking in general. Fortunately, the world also has text messaging. At the right time, a suggestive text message could build a sweet anticipation. I suggest we use texting, just like all other other forms of communication, to strengthen our entire connection, and not only for times of sexual motivation.

Be sure to remember, texted, written, recorded or photographed communications have the potential of becoming public, so only communicate with someone you trust, and be sure what you share would not cause grief if it was ever brought to the public.

If you like the idea of having this type of sexy communication, choose a time when you have already felt a positive connection with your lover for a span of days. Write whatever communicates your desire and shows an appreciation of his or her sexiness.

Sex does not just happen spontaneously in the bedroom. It builds.

CHAPTER FORTY-TWO
Clear Sharp Mind

Your natural connection to perfect knowledge can become clear when you let yourself feel good.
 Forgive yourself.
 Set yourself free.
 Proceed as free.
 Dualistic concepts (such as those regarded as *good* or *bad*) only want to become whole again. Relax out of old judgements.
 Give wholeness to your past by inviting it to relax into perfect acceptance and love. Give wholeness to your present and future in the same way. You can give wholeness to your experience of any concept.

CHAPTER FORTY-THREE
Best Health

Healthy habits help you be your most vibrant self. Eat natural foods like fruits and vegetables. Be active. Apply yourself with fitness, as fully as you can. Cut out any pollutant chemicals. Limit or cut out alcohol. Drink plenty of water.

As for staying hydrated, if you ever feel thirsty, you are likely already experiencing a slight degree of dehydration. I suggest you drink water before thirst ever becomes great. The physiological processes of your body and mind will be helped. With adequate water, your skin will even *smile*.

Well, this is advice we have all heard, right? Be assured, the choices are worthwhile. Your decision to live in a natural way will let your body and mind be capable and clear. Your self-esteem can strengthen. You will feel attractive and be discerning.

CHAPTER FORTY-FOUR
Whole Body

Strengthen your ability to feel more naturally sensual when you practice an activity that engages your whole body. Find at least one "whole body" activity that you enjoy, and do it regularly.

The activity should bring you into awareness of both the upper and lower portions of your body, simultaneously. This could be a form of dance, martial arts, yoga, or any such activity.

Do what you can.

Activities with free-form movement can give the added benefit of relaxing the mind. You let the feeling guide you. You feel your body, and interact with it.

This type of activity gives you skills that carry over into the bedroom. You become more connected with how you experience sensations.

CHAPTER FORTY-FIVE
Be Someone to Be

From an energetic viewpoint, sex is an invitation to actually *be* you. Proposing sex does more than just propose a physical activity. It asks the person to feel what you feel. You enter a unified state. With this understanding, you can make yourself appear sexy by being someone whose life feels good.

Decide to enjoy all areas of life as much as you can. Engage in a full and balanced life.

What do you enjoy doing? What will you like to study and learn? Can you spend increased time on projects supportive of your dreams? Do these! You win in the sense of producing a rich life experience. You also win in the sense of being seen as the best version of yourself, which is very attractive.

Your lover wants you to be in your glory. If you were not being your most glorious self, you had been led away from knowing who you really are.

Lighten up in order to move upward. Bring yourself to laughter. Put on a smile. Identify what brings you joy, and call those things to mind often.

CHAPTER FORTY-SIX

Truth

I invite you to express these powerful statements:
"I am above the influence of any concept or thing."
"I have what I need by being who I am."

CHAPTER FORTY-SEVEN
Be Whole

A sense of balance can result from making a positive choice. An athlete's physical achievement, for example, can open him or her to an unexpected, heightened spiritual capacity. Spiritual devotion may bring a person into a great appreciation of physical activities. The person who strengthens productivity also finds new depth to his or her moments of relaxation. These types of pleasant side effects reveal how every aspect of you will perfectly support the fulfillment of your being whole.

CHAPTER FORTY-EIGHT
Versions of You

Whether you want to be a stud, enchantress, dreamboat, knockout, or any other role, you can be! You be it as *you*. Emulating anyone else's version of such roles could become disorienting, so be the stud version of *you*, or the enchantress version of *you*, and so on.

CHAPTER FORTY-NINE
Real Eyes

With your eyes, you can show the true pleasure of being alive. Your eyes, then, invite the the other person to show you the same. Many people are traveling through a dull trance of responsibilities, awkward relationships, scrolling through feeds on their phones, and so on. The right person will welcome the depth you bring with your inviting look. He or she will be excited with the fun you awaken.

CHAPTER FIFTY
Initiate Intimacy

When the time is right for action, bring a playful smile and a powerful stare to your lover. If the person is shy, he or she may pretend to not recognize the intention of your look, and may even respond with defensively vague questions, such as "What?" or "What is it?" If this happens, go ahead and smile an even larger smile, and maintain your stare.

An intent stare shows desire. It brings your sexuality to the forefront.

Observe the reciprocating signals, as both partners reveal their desire for intimacy.

If you feel averse to initiating intimacy, even though you know you and your partner would like that kind of relationship, consider creating a Personal Commitment Phrase, or "PCP." This is a phrase you decide to speak to yourself when you need to commit to act. Speak it either aloud or in your mind.

I developed my "PCP" at an early age while skateboarding. If I felt afraid to roll forward into a trick, I would speak my phrase in my mind, "One, Two, I am brave, Three!" Then, based on the integrity I had built into the phrase, I was committed to attempt the skateboarding trick. In fact, I use the Personal Commitment Phrase on many days to get up out of bed when I would prefer to just snooze: "One, Two, I am brave, Three!" and I rise.

Initiate intimacy when the time is right. Do not miss out on the excitement you both crave.

CHAPTER FIFTY-ONE
Smile Sexy

A sexy smile is a relaxed smile. Relax your mind, body and face, and see how powerful your smile can become!

CHAPTER FIFTY-TWO
Feel What the Other Feels

Feel entirely what your lover feels. This is the highest form of eroticism.

Fellas, you may have noticed how women have historically provided men with almost no definitive advice about what they find pleasurable. Most men, on the other hand, could readily diagram what a man would enjoy. For women, though, pleasure is going to come when her lover will actually feel what she feels. He then knows exactly what to do.

Get your "thinking mind" out of the way. Feel so deeply that you begin to feel your lover's and your own pleasures as one.

CHAPTER FIFTY-THREE
Give

Believe that you will be seen as a wonderful gift to the right person. Your ability to give will bring your fullest pleasure.

In a relationship, when both give, both also receive.

Give during intimacy. Your experience becomes very rich when you let your loving expression flow into your partner. Every sexual motion is meant to give.

You can give the experience of an orgasm by intending for your presence to bring pleasure. There is not so much a formula to pleasure, as there is an intention.

Showing your own pleasure is also a gift to your lover.

To give through sex does not come at a cost to your own satisfaction. We are designed so that our own heightened pleasures align with those of our lover.

Both people give at the area of the genitals. Women also give at the breasts. All areas where we bring a concentrated awareness can give.

CHAPTER FIFTY-FOUR
Stillness

In foreplay or sex, be willing to bring your partner into total stillness.

Men, too often, feel a need to always "do something" sexually, such as have constant thrusting. A richer approach, though, is for a man to occasionally bring the activity with his lover into a sweet moment of stillness. This can feel like a moment outside of time. Of course, a transcendence of time can also occur during the normal thrusting rhythm, but it can happen especially powerfully in a moment of stillness.

Stillness is especially intense in foreplay. When you are close to touching, you take a moment to just feel your excitement. Penetrate with your eyes. Allow your bodies to communicate. You do not need to reference your thoughts at this point. Let the feeling build. Throb.

You can build excitement by pausing very briefly before any intimate act, like on your way to a kiss.

Do not overdo this, though. Too much sexual teasing would not make sense. This is purely a brief moment to honor the feeling of anticipation.

CHAPTER FIFTY-FIVE
Depressurize

An unfortunate concept has sometimes been included in communications about sex: "performance." I want to throw that word in the trash. Love never asks someone to perform. If you know someone who expects sex to be a performance, pass on having a relationship with him or her.

Keep an easy mind with a lover. Be willing to get intimate while having no expectation to have sex. Your lover should appreciate being close without feeling any pressure. Intimacy does not always need to mean phallic thrusts. Intimacy can sometimes mean being simply close and affectionate. Coincidentally, though, when you get close with no expectation for sex, your hottest sex may follow.

Expectations can produce worries, so let them go. One technique to let go of expectant, worried, or uncomfortable thoughts, is to pretend to watch them dissipate and blow away in a gust of wind, like so:

1. Imagine hearing the soft whistle of a blowing wind.
2. Watch any nervous thoughts break into tiny bits of dust, as they are gently blown away. You may even see them as bits of colors that whiten into a glowing light as they move away from you.

If you need anything from your lover in order to feel comfortable in sex, communicate this. Have what you need before having sex.

CHAPTER FIFTY-SIX
Perfect

You are perfect.
    Feel the warmth of self-love.

CHAPTER FIFTY-SEVEN
Role Play

Fantasy role play lets you act in ways you might not normally behave. It lets you play with situations you might not otherwise experience.

What would excite you in a role play story? Ask your lover this question. Ask yourself.

The roles you play — and the storyline, itself — can be decided as detailed or as loosely as you choose. You may like to leave room for some surprises.

The ideas are nearly endless. A person might like to assume the role of a teacher, celebrity, stranger, athlete, robot, innocent character, someone slutty… your imaginations write the experience. You may prefer to keep the characters fictitious, and not based on any actual people, so to avoid feelings of jealousy. Remember, you are not saying you would prefer sex with anyone other than your lover. You are simply creating a playful space together.

When planning your role play date, you can

decide together on the story, or individually write down ideas that you place into a jar and then choose one at random. Be sure you are both comfortable with the selection.

Put on some level of costume, whether you dress slightly different than normal, or very different. Are you intending to look cute, dignified, sexy, foreign, historic? Is makeup or a fragrance in order? Act the part. You can also dress up your environment in accordance with the fantasy. A prop or two may help you to stay in character.

Role play provides a level of freedom. For even greater freedom, you can place a story within a story. For example, you might pretend to be a couple actors who need to practice for a sexual movie scene. You begin your role play as the actors interacting professionally, then you transition in and out of the roles that the actors need to "rehearse." Pretending to be actors within your story can help an especially shy person to let loose.

Be free to speak in any way that excites you. Perhaps you have been shy in normal life, but within a fantasy you can run a dirty mouth.

CHAPTER FIFTY-EIGHT
Sex Not Required

We often interpret our life energy in a sexual way. The energy is sexual in the sense that it is creative. Physical sex can be a fun part of our creative expression. A primitive part of our minds may tend to go straight to that genetically well-worn path of physical sex as a place to experience sexiness. Sexiness, though, is the power we bring to our engagement with all aspects of life. Sexiness — as our natural expression — may not need to be sexual nor provocative, at all.

CHAPTER FIFTY-NINE

Live

Your decision to express as yourself will inform the world of what is right for you. It brings perfect opportunities into form.

You are important. Your expression is your gift to the world.

You can connect in meaningful ways. You can have relationships be how you desire them to be.

All of life is here to support your sweetest experience.

So…

                      Live your "Oh, my!"

About the Author

We hope you enjoyed this book.

Tyrus Gray is the host of the Delete Depression Podcast, which has been an active source of support for positive change and healing since 2012. He also creates the therapeutic music and audio programs at SacredSolfeggio.com

www.ingramcontent.com/pod-product-compliance
Lightning Source LLC
Chambersburg PA
CBHW070120110526
44587CB00016BA/2745